INSTRUCTIONS FOR CHILDREN
by
John Wesley

Edited by Rev. Dr. James T. Reuteler, Ph.D.

Summarize *Question* *Apply* *Witness*

COVENANT Bible Studies

INTRODUCTION

What follows are John Wesley's *Instructions for Children*. I was tempted to change MAN to PERSON, but decided against it. Sometimes that changes the meaning, and I am reluctant to change any of Wesley's meaning or content. I did change the spelling of a few words, such as HONOR for HONOUR. This does not change the meaning or content.

Wesley numbered some of what follows, but I have numbered everything in order make referring to a sentence or thought easier.

I didn't change Wesley's scheme for capitalization. While I don't know why he capitalizes so many words, I feared that he was expressing something that would be missed if I reduced his upper case words to lower case words.

It seems to me that Wesley was writing these instructions to older children, say somewhere between 12 and 16. The instructions on Hell would be disturbing to younger children; and perhaps, they would be disturbing to older children and adults as well. They are, however, Scriptural, even though they are disturbing.

Wesley did not place a heading at the top of each instruction, but the intent is obvious, and so, I inserted the topic headings. After dealing with God, the Fall, Redemption, the Means of Grace, Heaven, and Hell, Wesley deals with the following five topics:

1. God and the Soul of Man.
2. How to Regulate our Desires.
3. How to Regulate our Understanding.
4. How to Regulate our Joy.
5. How to Regulate our Practice.

Wesley begins with Theology, but quickly moves into the field of Ethics, and he ends with practical advice.

While Wesley wrote these instructions in the eighteenth century, they still speak to us today. If we think we can do better, then we ought to try. Our children stand in need of such guidance. So do adults. Perhaps adults will get more out these instructions than children.

James T. Reuteler, Ph.D.
Covenant Bible Studies
Aurora, Colorado
Jim@Reuteler.org
www.Jim.Reuteler.org

TABLE OF CONTENTS

INTRODUCTION 3

TO PARENTS AND SCHOOLMASTERS 7

SECTION I 9

    Lesson I and II: Of God 9
    Lesson III and IV: Of the Creation and Fall of Man 10
    Lesson V, VI, and VII: Of the Redemption of Man 11
    Lesson VIII and IX: Of the Means of Grace 13
    Lesson X and XI: Of Hell 14
    Lesson XII: Of Heaven 15

SECTION II 17

    Lesson I: Of GOD, and the Soul of Man 17
    Lesson II: Of GOD, and the Soul of Man 18
    Lesson III: Of GOD, and the Soul of Man 19
    Lesson IV: Of GOD, and the Soul of Man 20
    Lesson V: Of GOD, and the Soul of Man 21
    Lesson VI: Of GOD, and the Soul of Man 22

SECTION III 23

    Lesson I: How to Regulate our Desires 23
    Lesson II: How to Regulate our Desires 24
    Lesson III: How to Regulate our Desires 25
    Lesson IV: How to Regulate our Desires 26
    Lesson V: How to Regulate our Desires 27
    Lesson VI: How to Regulate our Desires 28
    Lesson VII: How to Regulate our Desires 30
    Lesson VIII: How to Regulate our Desires 31
    Lesson IX: How to Regulate our Desires 32
    Lesson X: How to Regulate our Desires 33
    Lesson XI: How to Regulate our Desires 34

SECTION IV 35

Lesson I: How to Regulate our Understanding 35
Lesson II: How to Regulate our Understanding 36
Lesson III: How to Regulate our Understanding 37
Lesson IV: How to Regulate our Understanding 38
Lesson V: How to Regulate our Understanding 39
Lesson VI: How to Regulate our Understanding 40
Lesson VII: How to Regulate our Understanding 42
Lesson VIII: How to Regulate our Understanding 43

SECTION V 45

Lesson I: How to Regulate our Joy 45
Lesson II: How to Regulate our Joy 46
Lesson III: How to Regulate our Joy 47
Lesson IV: How to Regulate our Joy 49
Lesson V: How to Regulate our Joy 50
Lesson VI: How to Regulate our Joy 51
Lesson VII: How to Regulate our Joy 52
Lesson VIII: How to Regulate our Joy 54
Lesson IX: How to Regulate our Joy 55

SECTION VI 57

Lesson I: How to Regulate our Practice 57
Lesson II: How to Regulate our Practice 59
Lesson III: How to Regulate our Practice 60
Lesson IV: How to Regulate our Practice 61
Lesson V: How to Regulate our Practice 63
Lesson VI: How to Regulate our Practice 64
Lesson VII: How to Regulate our Practice 66
Lesson VIII: How to Regulate our Practice 67
Lesson IX: How to Regulate our Practice 69
Lesson X: How to Regulate our Practice 70
Lesson XI: How to Regulate our Practice 71
Lesson XII: How to Regulate our Practice 72

TO ALL PARENTS AND SCHOOLMASTERS

1. I have laid before you in the following Tract, the true Principles of the Christian Education of Children. These should in all Reason be instilled into them, as soon as ever they can distinguish Good and Evil. If the Fear of the Lord is the Beginning of Wisdom, then it is certainly the very first thing they should learn. And why may they not be taught the Knowledge of God and the Knowledge of Letters, at the same time?

2. A great Part of what follows is translated from the French: Only it is here cast into another Form, and divided into Sentences, that it may be the more easily understood, either by the Teacher or the Learners. And although the great Truths herein contained, are more immediately addressed to Children, yet are they worthy the deepest Consideration, both of the oldest and wisest of Men.

3. Let them be deeply engraven in your own Hearts, and you will spare no Pains in teaching them to others. Above all let them not read or say one Line, without understanding and minding what they say.

4. Try them over and over; stop them short, almost in every Sentence. And ask them, "What was it you said last?" Read it again, "What do you mean by that?" So that, if it be possible, they may pass by nothing till it has taken some Hold upon them. By this Means they will learn to think as they learn to read. They will grow wiser and better every day. And you will have the Comfort of observing, that by the same Steps they advance in the Knowledge of these poor Elements, they will also grow in Grace, in the Knowledge of God, and our Lord Jesus Christ.

SECTION 1

Lesson I and II
Of God

1. How many Gods are there? One.
2. Who is God the Father, God the Son, and God the Holy Spirit[1]. These three are One
3. What is God? A Spirit.
4. What do you mean by a Spirit? One that cannot be seen or felt.
5. What sort of a Spirit is God. One that always was and always will be.
6. Where is God? Every where.
7. What does God know? Every Thing
8. What can God do? Whatever he will.
9. Does God love you? Yes. He loves every thing which he has made.
10. What has God made? Every thing, and in particular Man.

---

[1] Ghost.

Lesson III and IV
Of the Creation and Fall of Man

1. How did God make Man? His Body out of Dust, his Soul out of nothing.
2. Why did God make Man? To know, love, and be happy in God forever.
3. Where did God put the first Man and Woman? In the Garden of Paradise.
4. What Command did he give them there? Not to eat of the Tree in the Middle of the Garden.
5. Did they keep that Command? No, they did eat of it.
6. What Hurt did they bring on themselves hereby? Sin and Guilt, and Pain and Death.
7. Did their Sin hurt any beside themselves? Yes, all Men that came from them.
8. How did it hurt them? They are all born in Sin and Guilt, and subject to Pain and Death.
9. How are Men born in Sin? We are all born proud, self-willed, Lovers of the World, and not Lovers of God.

Lesson V, VI and VII
Of the Redemption of Man

1. By whom are we to be saved from Sin? By Jesus Christ, the Eternal Son of God.
2. What did he do to save us? He was made Man, and lived and died and rose again.
3. What may we gain by his living and dying for us? Forgiveness of Sins, and Holiness and Heaven.
4. When does God forgive our Sins? When we repent and believe in Christ.
5. What do you mean by Repenting? Being thoroughly convinced of our Sinfulness, Guilt, and Helplessness.
6. What is Believing, or faith? A Conviction of those unseen Things which God has told us in the Bible.
7. What is Faith in Christ? A Conviction that Christ has loved us, and given himself for me.
8. By whom is this wrought in us? By the Holy Spirit[2].
9. What is Holiness? The Love of God, and of all Mankind for God's sake.
10. Is he that believes and loves God saved from sin? Yes, from all sinful Tempers and Words and Works.
11. How is he saved from Pride? He is little and mean and safe and vile in his own Eyes.
12. How is he saved from Self will? His Heart continually says, "Lord, not as I will, but as thou wilt."
13. How is he saved from the Love of the World? He desires nothing but God.

---

[2] Ghost.

14. How is he saved from sinful Words? His Words always spring from the Grace of God, and are to minister Grace to the Hearers.

15. How is he saved from sinful Works? By the Spirit of God which dwelleth in him, whether he eats or drinks, or whatever he does, it is all to the Glory of God.

Lesson VIII and IX
Of the Means of Grace

1. What is Grace? The Power of the Holy Spirit[3], enabling us to behave and love and serve God.
2. How are we to seek this? In a constant and careful Use of the Means of Grace.
3. Which are the chief Means of Grace? The Lord's Supper, Prayer, Searching the Scriptures, and Fasting.
4. How often did the first Christians receive the Lord's Supper? Every Day. It was their daily Bread.
5. How often did they join in public[4] Prayers? Twice a Day, as many of them as could.
6. How often did they use private Prayer? Every Morning and Night, at least.
7. How did they search the Scriptures? They heard or read them every Day, and meditated therein Day and Night.
8. How often did the old Christians fast? Every Wednesday and Friday till Three in the Afternoon.
9. How long is every Christian to use all these Means of Grace? To his Life's End.

---

[3] Ghost.

[4] publick.

Lesson X, and XI
Of Hell

1. Where do Unbelievers go after Death? To Hell.
2. What sort of a Place is Hell? In a dark bottomless Pit, full of Fire and Brimstone.
3. How will they spend their Time there? In weeping and wailing and gnashing of Teeth.
4. Will both their Souls and Bodies be tormented? Yes, every Part of them at once.
5. How will their bodies be tormented? By lying in burning and flaming fire.
6. How will their Souls be tormented? By a Sense of the Wrath of God, by Pride, Self will, Malice and Envy, by Grief, Desire, Fear, Rage, and despair.
7. Who will be their tormentors? Their own Consciences, the Devils, and one another.
8. But will they have no Rest from Torment? No, not for one Moment, Day or Night.
9. How long will their Torment last? For ever and ever.

Lesson XII
Of Heaven

1. Where will Believers go after Death? To Heaven.
2. What sort of Place is Heaven? A Place of Light and Glory.
3. How will good Men live there? In Joy and Happiness, greater than they can now desire or think.
4. Will they suffer nothing there? No. They will have no Want, or Pain, or Sin.
5. What sort of Bodies will they have then? Spiritual Bodies, swifter than Lightning and brighter than the Sun.
6. But wherein will their chief Happiness lie? In the Enjoyment of God
7. How will they enjoy God? They will know, and love, and see God Face to Face.
8. How will they spend their Time? In singing Praise to God.
9. How long will this Happiness last? As long as God lives, that is, for ever and ever. Lord! bring me thither. Amen.

SECTION II

Lesson I
Of God, and of the Soul of Man

1. Take care you do not draw nigh to God with your Lips, while your Heart is far from him.
2. Never say anything to God which you do not mean.
3. Do not dare to tell a Lie to God for he sees all that is in your Heart.
4. Do you know what God is?
5. If you do not know God, how can you hope to please God?
6. Think on this. Mind it well. For God is here. He minds you, if you do not mind him.

Lesson II

Of God, and of the Soul of Man

1. God is an Eternal Spirit, without Beginning and without End.
2. He cannot be seen, nor fully known by Man.
3. He is Good, and all Good comes from him.
4. He has Power to do whatever he will.
5. He is Wise, knowing all Things, and doing all Things well.
6. He is happy, and cannot want any Thing.
7. He loves all Things which he has made, and Man above all.
8. It is his Will, that all Men should be favored, and come to the Knowledge of his Truth.
9. He is Swift, to give every Man according to his Works.
10. He is True, in his Promises, and in his Threatenings.
11. He is Merciful, forgiving the Sins of those who truly repent and believe.

Lesson III

Of God, and of the Soul of Man

1. No Man hath seen God at any Time. The Son of God, who is in the Bosom of the Father, he hath declared him unto us.

2. No one knoweth the Son of God, but the Father; and no one knoweth the Father, but the Son, and he to whom the Son will reveal him.

3. All our Reading, and the Things we hear either at Church, or any where else, cannot reveal God unto us.

4. All the Men in the World cannot give us the least Spark of the true Knowledge of God, or of the Things of God.

5. Only God himself can do this, by giving us his good Spirit.

6. He gives his Grace and his Light to those who pray earnestly for it.

7. He declares himself to those who do his Will, so far as they know it already.

Lesson IV

Of God, and of the Soul of Man

1. There is none Good, but One, that is, God..
2. Every Thing that is Good, comes from God alone, whether it be in Heaven or in Earth.
3. If there is any Thing good in any Man, it all comes from God.
4. Therefore He alone ought to be praised for it all.
5. All that we do without Him, without his Grace and his Help, is Evil.
6. Without God we can do nothing that is Good.
7. He that has not God, has nothing that is Good, and is more unhappy than any words can tell.

Lesson V

Of God, and of the Soul of Man

1. I know that God has Power, to keep what I commit to him, safe unto that Day.
2. Our Souls are now spoiled and destroyed by Sin.
3. No one can save us from our Sins, but God who has all Power.
4. Let us commit our Souls wholly to him, to do with them what he will, and as he will.
5. Then he will keep us by his Power, and defend us against every Thing that would hurt us.
6. He is able to deliver us from all Danger, and to keep our Souls unto that great Day.
7. And at that Day he will restore in Glory both our Bodies and Souls, and all that we had committed to his Charge.

Lesson VI

Of God, and of the Soul of Man

1. Do you know what your Soul is?
2. You have in you (though you cannot feel it) a Soul that will never die.
3. God made this, that he might come and dwell in it.
4. If God lives and dwells in your Soul, then he makes it like himself.
5. He makes the Soul in which he dwells. Good, Wise, Just, True, full of Love, and of Power to do well.
6. He makes it happy. For it is his Will, that your Soul should rejoice in him for ever. He made it for this very thing.
7. When a Soul desires God, and knows and enjoys him, then it is truly happy.
8. But when a Soul does not desire God, nor know and enjoy him, then it is truly miserable.

SECTION 1II

Lesson I
How to Regulate our Desires.

1. The Gate by which God and his holy Grace comes into us is the Desire of the Soul.
2. This is often called, the *Heart*, or the *Will*.
3. Unless our Desire be toward God, we cannot please him.
4. All our Knowledge, without this, does but make us the more like the Devil.
5. The Desire is to the Soul, what the Mouth and the Stomach are to the Body.
6. It is by the Mouth and the Stomach that the Body receives its Nourishment, whether good or bad.
7. That our Body may live, we must take care to put nothing but what is good into our Mouth or Stomach.
8. And, that our Soul may live, we must take care to desire nothing but what is good.

Lesson II
How to Regulate our Desires.

1. Desire was made for that which is Good, that is, for God, who is the only Good, and for his Will, from which every good Thing flows.
2. We ought to desire nothing but God, and that which is according to his holy Will.
3. And we ought to turn our Desire from every Thing beside.
4. For every Thing beside God and his Will, is evil.
5. Therefore no Man ought to follow his own Will.
6. As the Will of God is the Spring of all Good, to our own Will is the Spring of all Evil.
7. Take care, not to use yourself to do your Will.
8. No Soul can ever be saved, unless it renounces his own Will and its own Desires.
9. Father, let not my Will be done, but Thine.
10. We came into the World, not to do our own Will, but the Will of him that sent us.
11. If we are already accustomed to do our own Will, we must break that Custom without Delay.
12. O Lord, save us from our own Will, or we perish.

Lesson III
How to Regulate our Desires.

1. No one can do any Thing good of himself, without the Help of God.
2. All our own Desires are only evil continually.
3. Therefore no Man should desire to be esteemed, honored or praised by any Man.
4. And no one ought to praise or esteem himself.
5. Rather we ought to despise ourselves.
6. And we ought to desire to be thought by others, what we really are, that is, poor, weak, foolish, sinful Creatures.
7. Then should we find Help from God. For he resisteth the Proud, but giveth Grace to the Humble.
8. They who teach Children to love Praise, train them up for the Devil.
9. Praise is deadly Poison for the Soul; therefore never praise any one to his face.
10. Do not plant either in him or yourself that Pride of Heart which is an Abomination to the Lord.

Lesson IV
How to Regulate our Desires.

1. You are of yourself nothing but Sin, and deserve nothing but Hell.
2. Therefore you ought to be content, though you should have little or nothing in the World.
3. And you ought not to desire any thing more than you have, for you have now more than you deserve.
4. Choose therefore the worst and meanest Things; for even these are too good for such a Sinner.
5. To raise any other Desires in your Heart, is to prepare you for Hell-fire.
6. They that give you fine clothes[5], are giving your Soul to the Devil.
7. They that humor you, do not love you.
8. If your Father or Mother [is] giving you every Thing that you like, they are the worst enemies you have in the world.
9. By doing this, they make you Slaves to the Flesh, to Vanity and Corruption.
10. And to keep you as far from the Spirit of Christ, as the Devil himself can.

---

[5] cloaths

Lesson V
How to Regulate our Desires.

1. God is Power, Wisdom, Goodness itself.
2. Therefore we should desire, to praise and honor him as he deserves, and to please him in every thing.
3. The end for which we are born, is to praise and honor God.
4. And this we may do without ceasing, by continually lifting up our Hearts to him.
5. This is the continual Employment of the Angels of God in Heaven.
6. They sing Day and Night, to Him that sitteth upon the throne, and to the Lamb for ever and ever.
7. Holy, Holy, Holy, Lord God of Hosts! Let all the Earth be full of thy Glory.

Lesson VI
How to Regulate our Desires.

1. God is continually helping us, and pouring his benefits upon us.
2. All good things come from him, our Soul, our Body, our Life, our Parents, our Friends, and the good Angels that guard us.
3. The Earth on which we tread, the Air we breathe, the Sun which shines upon us, the Food that keep us alive, the Clothes[6] that cover us, the Fire that warms us, are all from him.
4. Therefore we should thank God, for all these Things, and for every one of them.
5. We ought to be thankful, even to a Man, when he does us any good.
6. How much more ought we to be thankful to God, who made that Man, and who does us good by him.
7. Thou art worthy, O Lord, our God, to receive Glory and Honor and Power.
8. Because thou hast created all Things, and for thy pleasure they are, and were created.
9. And God not only has done us all this Good, but he does us more and more Good continually.
10. For without his Goodness we and all the World should fall into nothing in a Moment.
11. We are just like a brittle Vessel, which if it were not always upheld, would fall at once and break in Pieces.
12. Therefore it should be our Desire to be always thanking God, because he is always blessing us.

---

[6] Cloaths.

13. O God, our Father, teach us to give thee Thanks, at all times, and for all Things, through Jesus Christ.

Lesson VII
How to Regulate our Desires.

1. Thus God has been helping us to this Day. And we have no less Need of his Help for the Time to come.
2. Above all, if we would be happy, we have Need of his Blessing upon our Souls.
3. These he gives to them who truly desire them, and to none else.
4. Therefore, let us desire of God, to give us his Grace, his good Spirit, and the Knowledge of himself.
5. Let us ask of him, a meek and quiet Spirit, a contented, humble, thankful Heart.
6. If any man lack Wisdom, let him ask of God, who giveth to all Men liberally, and it shall be given him.
7. Let us then take care, not to offend him, from whom we hope to receive so great Benefits.
8. And let us always be ready to do his Will, for if any Man honor God and do his Will, him he heareth.

Lesson VIII
How to Regulate our Desires.

1. But we have often offended God already, and so are unworthy of his Grace and Blessings.
2. Therefore we ought with earnest Desire to ask of God to forgive our past Sins, for the Sake of his Son who died for us, and to keep us from them for the Time to come.
3. These Desires ... are what we commonly call Prayer.
   a. To praise God, and his Power, Wisdom and Goodness,
   b. to thank him for all his Benefits;
   c. To ask his Grace, that so we may please him; and
   d. To beg his Mercy, for the Pardon of our Sins,
4. We never pray, but when we have really these Desires in our Heart.
5. If we say ever so many Words, without having these Desires, we are but like Parrots before God.
6. Beware of this, of drawing nigh unto God with your Lips, while your Heart, (that is, your Desire) is far from him.

Lesson IX
How to Regulate our Desires.

1. What do you mean, when you pray to God, in the name of Jesus Christ?
2. The bare saying these Words signifies nothing. It is only mocking God, if you do not know what you say.
3. We were all under the Wrath and under the Curse of God, when Jesus Christ, the Son of God, died for us.
4. And for his Sake, if we really believe in him, God is now reconciled to us.
5. Therefore all our Trust should be in Jesus Christ, whenever we pray to God for any Thing.
6. For God would not hear us at all, but for the Sake of the Blood of Christ shed for us.
7. Therefore we ought to pray always, with an Eye to him, looking unto Jesus.
8. And our Desires should all spring from his Grace, and be agreeable to his Desires.
9. Then he offers our Desires, as his own, to God his Father, before whose Throne he stands
10. And God can refuse nothing to the Desires and the Merits of his well-beloved Son.
11. When therefore you pray in the Name of Jesus Christ, it is as if you should say, "Lord, I offer thee the Desires which are wrought in me by the Grace of Jesus Christ.
12. I pray, that thou wilt unite them to the Desires of thy Son, and regard them as his, who is pleading for me.
13. And grant me what I thus desire, for his Sake, for thy own Glory and my Salvation.

Lesson X
How to Regulate our Desires.

1. Pray to God in such Words as come from your Heart:
2. It may be, such as these:
3. My God, Thou art Good. Thou art Wise. Thou art Powerful. Be thou praised forever.
4. Give me Grace, to love and obey thee
5. My God, I thank thee, for making and for redeeming me.
6. My God, I thank thee for giving me Meat and clothes[7], and for promising to give me thy Love for ever.
7. My God, forgive me all my Sins, and give me thy good Spirit.
8. Let me believe in thee with all my Heart, and love thee with all my Strength.
9. Let me be always looking unto Jesus Christ, who is pleading for me at thy Right-hand.
10. Give me Grace not to do my own Will but thine.
11. Make me content with every Thing. The least of all the Good Things thou givest me, is far more than I deserve.
12. Give me. O my Lord, a lowly Heart.
13. Let me not think myself better than any one.
14. Let me despise myself, and look upon myself as the very worst of all.
15. Let me hate all Praise. Thou alone, O my God art worthy to be praised.

---

[7] Cloaths.

Lesson XI
How to Regulate our Desires.

1. The best Prayer in the World is the Prayer which our Lord Jesus Christ himself has taught us.
2. Our Father which art in Heaven,
3. Hallowed be thy Name,
4. Thy Kingdom come,
5. Thy Will be done in Earth as it is in Heaven,
6. Give us this Day our daily Bread, and
7. Forgive us our trespasses, as we forgive them that trespass against us,
8. And Lead us not into Temptation, but deliver us from Evil,
9. For thine is the Kingdom and the Power and the Glory, forever and ever. Amen,
10. Do you understand what you have said now?
11. How dare you say to God, you know not what (to say).
12. Do not you know, that this is no Prayer, unless you speak it from your Heart?
13. God is not pleased with your saying these Words, unless there is in your Heart at the same Time a real Desire, that God should be
    a. Known and esteemed,
    b. Honored and praised,
    c. Obeyed by all Men.
    d. That he should feed your Souls with his Grace and his Love,
    e. That he should forgive you your past Sins, and
    f. That he should keep you for the Time to come, from all Sin and from the Snares of the Devil.

SECTION IV

Lesson I
How to Regulate Our Understanding

1. Our understanding was made for Truth, that is, for God himself, for his Word and his Works.

2. Therefore we should not desire to know any Thing but God, and what he has spoken and done for his own Glory.

3. Accordingly, Lying is the most abominable of all Things. The Devil is a Liar and the Father of it.

4. We should not desire to know, what Men say and do. It is Folly and Vanity.

5. Curiosity is good for nothing.

6. It fills our Mind with Darkness, and makes us senseless and unfit for the Light of God.

7. What a Loss is this, to fill those Vessels with Filth and Dung, which were made to receive the pure Light of God.

Lesson II
How to Regulate Our Understanding

1. That Eye of the Understanding, which should see God, is quite shut in all Men since the Fall.

2. We are born quite blind to God and the Things of God.

3. And it is God alone who can open the Eyes of our Soul, to see and know spiritual Things.

4. We could not see or know the Sun, the Earth, or any other of the Things of this World, if God had not given us bodily Eyes.

5. And we can never know the Things of God, if God does not restore the spiritual Eyes of our Soul.

6. This he does for those and those only, who flee from Evil, and learn to do Good.

7. Give me Understanding, O Lord, and I will keep thy Law. Yea I will keep it with my whole Heart.

8. Open thou mine Eyes, that I may see the wondrous Things of thy Law.

9. Ti'l God opens our Eyes, to see the Things above, we must believe what God has told us, though we see it not.

10. But we must not believe what the World tells us about the things of God, for all Men who have not the Spirit, are blind and Liars.

11. We must trust in God, as to those Things which as yet we cannot comprehend.

12. And wait and desire, that he would open the Eyes of our Understanding, and give us his Light, that we may see all Things clearly.

Lesson III
How to Regulate Our Understanding

1. A blind Man, though he could reason ever so well, yet could not by this Means, either know or see the Things of the World.

2. And with all his Reason he could have only very dark, gross, nay and false Conceptions of them.

3. In like Manner, though all the Men in the World should reason with all their Might concerning them, yet could they not by this Means know either God or the Things of God.

4. Nay, with all their Reason they could only have dark, foolish, false Conceptions of them.

5. Before God can be known, he must give other Eyes to the Soul, and other Light than a Man can give.

6. We may paint the Sun or Fruits in a Picture, but the painted Sun cannot warm, or give us Light.

7. And those painted Fruits cannot nourish us, nor give us any Strength.

8. Just so we may draw Pictures, as it were, in our Mind, of God and of the Things of God.

9. But these Pictures can give us no true Light. Neither can they nourish our Souls, or give us any Strength to serve God.

10. They are only dead Shadows, cold and empty, barren and unfruitful.

11. We can build nothing upon them but the Wind, which serves only to puff Men up, and to drive each against the other in endless Disputes, till they burst of themselves, or dash in Pieces one against another.

Lesson IV
How to Regulate Our Understanding

1. Our Understanding or Reason, without the Grace and Supernatural Light of God, is like a blind Man, who draws wild, random Pictures of Things he never saw, nor can see.
2. The Natural Man discerneth not the Things of the Spirit of God.
3. They are Foolishness unto him, neither can he know them, because they are spiritually discerned.
4. No one knoweth the Things of God but the Spirit of God and he to whom God revealeth them by his Spirit.
5. Offer therefore your Understanding to God with a sincere Desire to do his Will only.
6. And pray him earnestly, to give you his Light, and to open the Eyes of your Soul.

Lesson V
How to Regulate Our Understanding

1. Endeavor to see God in all Things, and to give a Reason for every Thing, from the Perceptions of God.
2. For Example, Why was the World made? To show the Goodness, and Wisdom, and Power of God.
3. Why do Men die? Through the Justice of God.
4. Men having abused the Life he gave, it was just to take it away.
5. Why is it our Duty to obey our Parents? Because it is the Will of God.
6. Why ought we not to return Evil for Evil? Because God would have us do like him who is continually doing good to us, even when we ourselves do evil.
7. Why may we not despise or judge of our Neighbor? Because God is the judge of us all.
8. Thus we should accustom ourselves to have God always before our eyes, and to walk continually in his Presence.
9. Thus every Thing may show us the Power, Wisdom or Goodness, the Truth, Justice or Will of God.
10. And so every Thing may show us, the Weakness, Ignorance, Folly and Wickedness of Men.

Lesson VI
How to Regulate Our Understanding

1. What do you believe of God?

2. I believe in God the Father, Almighty, Maker of Heaven and Earth,

3. And in Jesus Christ, his only Son, our Lord, Who was conceived by the Holy Spirit[8], born of the Virgin May;

4. Suffered under Pontus Pilate, was crucified, dead and buried, he descended into Hell.

5. The third Day he rose again from the Dead.

6. He ascended into Heaven, and sitteth at the Righthand of God the Father Almighty.

7. From thence he shall come to judge the Quick and the Dead.

8. I believe in the Holy Spirit[9],

9. The Holy Catholic Church,

10. The Communion of Saints,

11. The Forgiveness of Sin,

12. The Resurrection of the Body, and the Life everlasting.

13. You may learn from these Words (1) To believe in God, the Father, who is Powerful, and Wise and Good, who made you and all Things, Visible and Invisible, Temporal and Eternal.

14. You may learn, (2) To believe in God the Son, who lived and died to redeem you and all Mankind.

---

[8] Ghost.

[9] Ghost.

15. And (3) To believe in God the Holy Spirit[10], who restores fallen Man to the Image of God in which he was made.

---

[10] Ghost.

Lesson VII
How to Regulate Our Understanding

1. All which come to this: Almighty God, the Maker of all Things, made Man to this Intent that desiring God alone, God might fill him with his Knowledge, with his Love and Joy and Glory for ever.

2. But Man turned his Desire from God and his Will, and so became both guilty, wicked and miserable.

3. The Son of God was made Man, lived and died and rose again, to buy Forgiveness for us, and to show us how we ought to renounce our own Will and Desires, and to give ourselves up to the holy Will of God.

4. Thus the Holy Spirit[11] works in us, enlightening our Understanding, and filling our Souls with a divine Peace and Joy.

5. Hereby we are joined again with all that is holy, either in Earth or Heaven.

6. We rejoice together with them in the common Salvation, in the Benefits and Grace of Jesus Christ.

7. And after the Body is dead and risen again, we shall live together in eternal Glory.

---

[11] Ghost.

Lesson VIII
How to Regulate Our Understanding

1. We cannot now comprehend, how these three are one, God the Father, the Son and the Holy Spirit[12].
2. But though we do not comprehend it, yet we believe it, because God has said it.
3. The true Knowledge of all the Things of God is wrought in our Souls by his Holy Spirit.
4. This is a Saving Knowledge, when it works by Love and brings us to imitate God.
5. So we are taught by St. Paul, Be ye Followers of God, as dear children, and walk in Love, as Christ also hath loved us, and given himself for us.
6. For every one that loveth[13] is born of God and knoweth God.
7. But he that loveth not, knoweth not God for God is Love.
8. So likewise, if any Man say, he knows Jesus Christ, and keepeth not his Commandments, he is a Liar, and the Truth is not in him.
9. We then savingly[14] Know God, the Father, the Maker of all Things, when we love him with obedient Reverence.
10. When we confidently give ourselves up into his Hands, and rely on his Providence.
11. And when we imitate his Goodness in all Things, and toward all Men,

---

[12] Ghost.

[13] The following is added here: (faith st. John).

[14] Unclear.

12. We then livingly know God the Redeemer, when we live as those whom he has bought with his Blood.

13. And when all our Tempers, and Words and Actions show, that he has redeemed us from the present evil World.

14. We savingly[15] know God the Sanctifier, when we are holy as he is holy.

15. When he hath purified both our Hearts and Lives by Faith, so that we continually see and love God.

---

[15] Unclear.

SECTION V

Lesson I
How to Regulate our Joy.

1. Men are poor, ignorant, foolish Sinners, that will shortly rot in the Earth.
2. And all that is in the World is perishable and vain, and will soon be destroyed by Fire.
3. Therefore we ought by no means to place our Joy and Delight on any of these Things.
4. Neither ought we to rejoice or delight in pleasing Man, who will quickly turn to Dust.
5. Nor in being handsome, or well dressed, or well provided with all Things. For all this will perish for ever.
6. God alone is Great Good, and the Giver of all good Things.
7. Therefore we ought to rejoice and delight in him alone, and in the fulfilling of his good and holy Will.
8. And we should not accustom ourselves to this to rejoice and delight in God and his holy Will.

Lesson II
How to Regulate our Joy.

1. For Example. We should rejoice, that we have for our true Father, an Eternal and Almighty God.
2. We should rejoice, that this God has made us, to fill us with divine and eternal Joy.
3. That is, if we will believe in Jesus, and do his holy Will.
4. If we love and obey him, and not love either the Honors, Riches or Pleasures that pass away like a Dream.
5. And this we may do, by the Power of his Grace, by the Holy Spirit[16] which he is ready to give unto us.
6. We should rejoice, that God is happy and glorious in himself, that he is greater than we can think.
7. That he knows every thing, and can do every thing.
8. That he is just and good, that he is true in all his Promises, and wise to teach and govern us as well.
9. We should rejoice, that God alone deserves to be desired, known, loved, praised and glorified for ever.
10. We should rejoice that the Son of God took our Nature upon him, in order to take us with him to Heaven for ever.
11. And that even now, he will come and dwell in our Heart, if we desire it, and believe in him and do his Will.

---

[16] Ghost

Lesson III
How to Regulate our Joy.

1. When any thing is done according to the Will of God, we ought to rejoice in it.
2. But when any thing is done according to our own Will, we ought not to rejoice, but to be sorry for it.
3. Therefore we ought to be greatly troubled and deeply sorry, for the Sins committed against God, whether by ourselves or others.
4. For in sinning we follow our own Will, and despise the holy Will of God.
5. Likewise, when any one praises us if we were wise, we should be ashamed and sorry, and should say,
6. O Lord, thou art good, and thou alone. Thou alone art worthy to be praised.
7. O Lord, it is a shameful Theft for a poor Creature to take to itself, the Esteem and Praise which belong to thee only.
8. On the contrary, when we are despised or ill used[17], or when we have not things as we would have, we should rejoice.
9. We should take all as from the Hand of God, and be well content, saying unto him, O Lord, I deserve nothing but Pain and Contempt, I rejoice that thy Justice gives me what I deserve.
10. I desire to thank thee for it with all my Heart, and to rejoice that thy holy Will is done upon me.
11. It is thy Will, that we should be like Christ; and he was despised and hated of Men.

---

[17] Unclear

12. He lived in Contempt, and Want, and Pain. O let me rejoice to tread in his Steps.

13. Let me be content, let me rejoice to suffer with him, that I may reign with him.

Lesson IV
How to Regulate our Joy.

1. One that is sick, if he is wise, will rejoice to take a good Medicine, be it ever so bitter.

2. Especially if he knows it is given him by a wise Physician, and that it will restore his bodily Health.

3. In like manner, if we are wise, we shall rejoice to take what God sends us, be it ever so bitter.

4. For we are sure, it is given us by the wise Physician of our Souls, in order to restore them to Health and Life everlasting.

5. On the contrary, It would be Folly and Madness in a sick Man, to rejoice in taking the Things that pleased his Taste, though they would kill him.

6. And the same Folly and Madness it is in us, to rejoice in taking the Things that please our corrupt Will.

7. Because the End of these Things is Death, even the destroying both Body and Soul in Hell.

Lesson V
How to Regulate our Joy.

1. When you are glad of any Thing that is given you, be sure to remember, that all this comes from God.
2. Therefore thank him for it, and think in yourself, God has a thousand and a thousand Times more than this, to give to them that love and obey him.
3. And be ready to leave all these little Things, whenever it is his Will.
4. If any one says to you, See what a pretty Thing here is, or, Look, here is a fine Thing for you, they are Fools, and know not what they do.
5. This is the Way, to make you fond of such foolish Things. But if you love these, you cannot love God.
6. If any one ever said to you, "Did it hurt you? Give me a Blow[18] for it." They were then teaching you to serve the Devil.
7. For this was teaching you to revenge yourself, and to revenge ourselves is serving the Devil.
8. If any one used to say to you, when you did any thing, "It was not my Child[19], was it? Say it was me.."
9. Then they were leading you the Way to Hell. For all Liars go to Hell.
10. And whoever they are that teach their Children Lying, Pride, or Revenge, they offer their Sons and their Daughters unto Devils.

---

[18] Unclear.

[19] Unclear.

Lesson VI
How to Regulate our Joy.

1. Above all, beware of the Love of Money. For it is the Root of all Evil.
2. Money is now the God of this World. The aim of Men is to get and keep this. And herein they place their Welfare and Joy.
3. This is an Idolatry no less damnable, than that of the Heathen World.
4. There would be little or rather no Use for Money, if Love governed the World.
5. And even now, Money is good for nothing, but as it is a Means of procuring among Men of the World, the things needful to sustain Life.
6. Neither ought we to desire it any farther, than as it is needful for this End.
7. God to whom it belongs (as do all Things) will require us to give a strict Account of it.
8. His Will is, that when we have used what is needful of it for ourselves, we should give all the rest to the Poor, and for his Glory.
9. Do not use yourself therefore to lay it up, but give what you can spare to the Poor.
10. Or else buy a little Meat or Clothes[20] for them, or some good Book for their Instruction.
11. And rejoice when you use your Money thus because that is for the Glory of God.

---

[20] Cloaths.

Lesson VII
How to Regulate our Joy.

1. Joy was made for God. Therefore we are taught in his Word to rejoice in the Lord always.
2. We should look upon God and his Grace as a great Treasure, and thence we may learn, now to rejoice in him.
3. When we posses a vast Treasure, so that we cannot possibly lose it, then our Joy is perfect.
4. Such will be the Joy of the Saints in Heaven, because then they cannot possibly lose this Treasure any more.
5. But when we posses a vast Treasure in such a manner that we may lose it every Moment, it is plain that our Joy therein should be tempered with a very serious Fear.[21]
6. And so it is with us. We may lose the Grace of God, yea every Moment, by divers Ways.
7. We may lose it by our own willful Sins, by our Negligence, or by our Presumption.
8. To these we are tempted continually, by an infinite Number of malicious and subtle Enemies.
9. These surround us at all Times and in all Places, and they never rest Day or Night.
10. Day and Night the Devil goeth about as a roaring Lion, seeking whom he may devour.
11. Therefore blessed is the Man that feareth always.
12. And accordingly the same Apostle who teaches to rejoice in the Lord always,

---

[21] Unclear

13. Teaches us at the same time, to work out our own Salvation with Fear and Trembling.
14. And so St. Peter, Speaking to those who rejoice in Christ, with Joy unspeakable and full of Glory;
15. Advises them to remember him, who would judge them according to their Works, and to pass the Time of their sojourning in Fear.

Lesson VIII
How to Regulate our Joy.

1. If we have lost this great Treasure by our own Fault, we have nothing in its Place but Poverty and Misery.

2. But God has promised, to give it to us again, if we are thoroughly sensible of our Loss.

3. If we repent, bring forth Fruits meet for Repentance, and truly believe in Jesus Christ.

4. So there is room for us all to rejoice in Hope, yet with a lively Sense of our past Sins, and present Misery.

5. For to such alone is the Promise made. Thus faith, the Lord, To this Man will I look, even to him that as Poor, and of a contrite Spirit, and that trembleth at my Word.

6. And our Lord says, Blessed are they that mourn, for they shall be comforted.

7. A broken and a contrite Heart, O God, thou wilt not despise.

Lesson IX
How to Regulate our Joy.

1. Even Religious Joy, if it be not thus mixed with Fear, will soon be a mere Nest of Self Love.
2. It will cover the greatness of our Corruption, and so hinder us from seeking to be cured of it.
3. It will make us carnally perfume, that we have the Treasure of Grace, while indeed we are far from it.
4. So the Church of Laodicea said, I am rich and increased in Goods, and have Need of nothing.
5. But Christ answered, Thou knowest not that thou art wretched and miserable, and poor, and blind, and naked.
6. And it is to such that he says, Woe unto you that are rich, for you have received your Consolation.
7. Woe unto you that are full, for ye shall hunger.
8. Woe unto you that laugh now, for ye shall mourn and weep.
9. These are they to whom St. James says, Be afflicted, and mourn and weep.
10. Let your Laughter be turned to Mourning, and your Joy to Heaviness.
11. Blessed is the Man that feareth the Lord, for the Fear of the Lord is the Beginning of Wisdom.
12. Therefore, learn to serve the Lord in Fear, and to rejoice in him with Reverence.

SECTION V1

Lesson I
How to regulate our Practice

1. Our Body and our Life belong to God. Therefore we ought to dispose of them according to his Will, not according to our own.

2. Our own Will naturally inclines to our own Profit, our own Honor, and our own Pleasure. And thus it begets in us the deadly Vices of Covetousness, Pride and Sensuality.

3. These hinder the Workings of God in us, and the Salvation of our Souls.

4. Therefore we ought to accustom ourselves, with God's Help, to deny ourselves in all things.

5. We should accustom ourselves to do all we do in a Spirit of Charity, and for the God of others.

6. In a Spirit of Humanity, without any Design or Desire of being esteemed.

7. And in a Spirit of Penitence, without any regard to our own Pleasure either of Body or Mind.

8. In all Things we should aim at being made conformable to our crucified Savior.

9. This is the true Spirit of the Christian Life and Practice. This is true Christianity.

10. But it is wholly opposite to the Spirit of the World and of corrupt Nature;

11. By which, alas, one suffers one's self to be so softly drawn into Hell, and drops falling[22] into everlasting Perdition.

---

[22] Unclear.

Lesson II
How to regulate our Practice

1. It is the Will of God, that we should do nothing but to please him.
2. It is his Pleasure, to be glorified by our Salvation.
3. His Glory should be our supreme, absolute, and universal End.
4. The Glory of God is advanced in this Life, when we give ourselves up to Jesus Christ.
5. Then his Power works through us many Holy Actions; for which he alone is to be honored and praised.
6. Without me...ye can do nothing. But he that abideth in me bringeth forth much Fruit.[23]
7. Herein is my Father glorified, that ye bear much Fruit.
8. This is to be understood of all Sorts of Actions and Things for every Thing we do, is to be done to the Glory of God.
9. And nothing can be done well but in the Name that is, in the Strength and through the Blessing of Jesus Christ.
10. Whether ye eat or drink, or whatever ye do, do all to the Glory of God.
11. Whatsoever ye do in Word or Deed, do all in the Name of the Lord Jesus.

---

[23] Wesley adds "faith our Lord" in the sentence.

Lesson III
How to regulate our Practice

1. So, for Example, you eat and drink to the Glory of God, and in the Name of Jesus Christ, when we are enabled by him to do it, on a right Principle and in a right Manner, so as to say to him from the heart.
2. Suffer me not, O Lord, to eat and drink, like a brute Beast, only by a brutal Appetite.
3. Much less do thou suffer me to follow herein the Motions of my corrupt Nature.
4. But grant me, through the Spirit of thy Son, to eat and drink so much as is needful to support my Life.
5. And let me spend that Life wholly in blessing thee, and in loving and obeying thee.
6. So likewise you speak to the Glory of God, and in the Name of Jesus Christ, when by his Strength you say nothing but what is guided by him, and directed according to his Will.
7. When you speak nothing but what is needful and proper to give Men good Thoughts, and turn them from such as the wicked and vain.
8. And thus, in all Things, let this be your single Aim, That God may be glorified through Jesus Christ.

Lesson IV
How to regulate our Practice

What are the Ten Commandments of God?

1. Thou shalt have none other Gods but me.

2. Thou shalt not make to thyself any graven Image, nor the Likeness of any Thing that is in Heaven above, or in the Earth beneath, or in the Water under the Earth. Thou shalt not bow down to them nor worship them for I the Lord thy God, am a jealous God, and visit the Sins of the Fathers upon the Children, unto the third and fourth Generation of them that hate me, and show[24] Mercy into Thousands of them that love me and keep my Commandments.

3. Thou shalt not take the Name of the Lord thy God in vain, for the Lord will not hold him guiltless that taketh his Name in vain.

4. Remember that thou keep holy the Sabbath Day. Six Days shalt thou labor and do all that thou hast to do, but the Seventh Day is the Sabbath of the Lord thy God. In it thou shalt do no manner of Work, thou and thy Son and thy Daughter, thy Manservant and thy Maidservant, thy Cattle and the Stranger which is within thy Gates. For in six Days the Lord made Heaven and Earth, the Sea and all that in them is, and rested the seventh Day, therefor the Lord blessed the Sabbath day and hallowed it.

5. Honor thy Father and thy Mother, that thy Days may be long in the Land which the Lord thy God giveth thee.

6. Thou shalt do no Murder.

7. Thou shalt not commit Adultery.

8. Thou shalt not steal.

---

[24] shew

9. Thou shalt not bear false Witness agains thy Neighbor.
10. Thou shalt not covet thy Neighbor's House, thou shalt not covet thy Neighbor's Wife, nor his Servant, nor his Maid, nor his Ox, nor his Ass, nor any thing that is his.

Lesson V
How to regulate our Practice

1. Consider. The Law of God is a spiritual Law. Therefore all these Commandments are to be spiritually understood.
2. The first Commandment means, Thou shalt not think, believe, or own any Thing to be God but me.
3. Thou shalt not fear any Thing but me.
4. Thou shalt not seek after Witches or Wizards, or practice any such Abomination.
5. Thou shalt not put Trust in any Creature.
6. Thou shalt not love any thing but me, or for my Sake.
7. God likewise herein commands thee. to believe in him, and to acknowledge him in all thy Ways.
8. He commands thee, to thank him for all thou hast, and to make him thy only Fear and thy only Dread.
9. To be in the Fear of the Lord all the Day long, and to trust in him with all thy Heart.
10. To desire him alone, to rejoice in him always, and to love him with all thy Heart and with all thy Soul.
11. The second Commandment teaches us, not to fancy that God is like the Thoughts or Imaginations of our dark Reason.
12. It teaches us also, not to worship or bow to any Image or picture, but to glorify God both with our Bodies and with our Spirits.

Lesson VI
How to regulate our Practice

1. If we will keep the third Commandment,
2. We must never swear falsely; and if we have sworn to do any thing, we must surely do it.
3. We must never use the Name of God at all, but with Reverence and godly Fear.
4. We must not value ourselves upon his Name, his Covenant, or the Knowledge of him, in vain.
5. That is, without profiting thereby, without bringing forth suitable Fruits.
6. We must not cover over our own Will, or Passions, or Designs, with the holy Name of God, of his Truth, or his Glory.
7. By the Fourth Commandment you are taught, to do no worldly Business on the Lord's Day.
8. But to spend it wholly in Prayer, Praise, hearing or reading the Word of God, and other Works of Piety and Charity.
9. The fifth Commandment teaches you these Things.
10. Show all Lowliness and Reverence to your Father and Mother, and do whatever either of them bids you.
11. If need be, relieve them, and never let them want any thing you can help them to.
12. Esteem the Ministers who are over you in the Lord very highly in love for their Work-sake.
13. Obey them, and submit yourselves to them; for they watch over your Souls.
14. Honor the King. Obey Magistrates. Pray for Kings, and all that are in Authority.

15. If you have a Master or Mistress, be obedient to them in Singleness of Heart, as unto Christ.

Lesson VII
How to regulate our Practice

1. The Sixth Commandment forbids not only the Killing or Hurting any one, but all Anger, hatred, Malice or Revenge.
2. It forbids all provoking Words, all Strife and Contention, all Gluttony and Drunkenness.
3. The Seventh Commandment forbids, not only all outward Uncleanness, but even the Looking on a Woman to lust after her.
4. It forbids also the suing any Thing, merely to please ourselves. For this is a Kind of spiritual Fornication.
5. The Eighth Command forbids not only the taking from another what is his, either openly secretly.
6. But likewise the stealing from God (to whom they all belong) either our Affections, or our Time, or our Goods, or our Labor, by employing any of them otherwise than for him.
7. The Ninth Commandment requires us, to put away all lying, and to speak the Truth from our Heart.
8. It requires us to speak Evil of no Man, but to put away all back-biting and Tale bearing.[25]
9. It requires us also, to judge no Man, that we be not judged, but to leave every one to God, the Judge of all.
10. The Tenth Commandment requires us to be content with what we have, and to desire nothing more.

---

[25] Gossiping.

Lesson VIII
How to regulate our Practice

1. These are those Laws of God, so wonderful and holy, of which David speaks so often with such Love and Admiration.
2. These all the Scriptures recommend as the Spring of Life, the Light of the Heart, the Treasure of Souls. Yea, our Lord calls them Life everlasting. John 12:50.
3. These the Holy Spirit has promised to write in the Hearts of those that truly believe in Jesus.
4. They may all be summed up in three.
   a. To love God,
   b. To love Jesus Christ himself, his Cross and his Tribulations, his Reproach, the Fellowship of his Sufferings, and the being made conformable to his Death.
   c. To love our Neighbor.
5. Our Heart therefore should always be full of Reverence for these. The Love of them should be fixed in the very Marrow of our Bones.
6. We should labor after this, by earnest Prayer, by reading, and by meditating on those deep Words.
7. The Law of the Lord is an undefiled Law (the Law of Love) converting the Soul: The Testimony of the Lord is sure, and giveth Wisdom unto the Simple.
8. The Statutes of the Lord are right, and rejoice the Heart; the Commandment of the Lord is pure, and giveth Light unto the Eyes.
9. The Fear of the Lord is clean and endureth for ever; the Judgments of the Lord are true, and righteous altogether.

10. More to be desired are they than Gold, yea than much fine Gold, sweeter also than Honey and the Honey comb.

11. Moreover, by them is thy Servant taught, and in keeping of them is great Reward.

Lesson IX
How to regulate our Practice

1. In a Word with regard to God, always live and act, as being in the Presence of God.
2. Remember, he is continually looking upon you.
3. And he will bring into Judgment, all that you have done, said, or thought, whether it be good or evil.
4. For all which you will be either rewarded or punished everlastingly.
5. Never fail to pray to God, Morning and Evening, as well as before and after you eat or drink.
6. Often lift up your Heart to God at other Times, particularly before any Work or Business.
7. Desire his Blessing and Help, and afterwards give him Thanks, and offer it up to God and his Glory.
8. Hear the Truths of God with Attention and Reverence, whether at home or at Church.
9. But do not think you have served God, barely because you have heard them, or have got them by Heart.
10. Pray to God to give you a true[26] Understanding of them, and to enliven them by the Working of his Spirit.
11. Pray him to give you an humble, submissive, simple and obedient Heart.
12. As to your Father and Mother, and Superiors, Pray to God for them, love and reverence them, obey them without murmuring, even in those Things which do not please you, unless they are plainly Sins.
13. Do nothing without their Knowledge, or without their Leave.

---

[26] Unclear.

Lesson X
How to regulate our Practice

1. With regard to your Neighbors, and your Companions,

2. Pray to God for them also, wish them well as you do to yourself, and do to them as you would have them do to you.

3. Think every one better than yourself.

4. Live in Peace with them, help them, if they have done you Wrong, forgive them, and pray heartily to God for them.

5. With regard to yourself,

6. Pray to God that you may always think meanly of yourself.

7. Eat nothing between Meals.

8. At your Meals eat moderately, of whatever is given you, whether you like it or not.

9. Desire nothing fine. Do not desire Abundance of any Thing. Be content with a little.

10. Employ your Time as you are directed. Never be doing nothing. Idleness tempts the Devil to tempt you.

11. Whatever you do, do it as well as you can.

12. Do not dispute, do not contradict any one, do not talk unless there be a Necessity.

13. Do not seek to excuse yourself when you have done wrong, but be always ready to confess your Fault, both to God and Man.

14. For God will not forgive your Sins, so long as you strive to excuse it.

Lesson XI
How to regulate our Practice

1. If you do any Thing well, thank God for it, and say,
2. I praise thee, O Lord, for giving me Grace to do this. Without thee I can do nothing but Evil.
3. And take Care not to value yourself upon it. If you do, it destroys your Soul.
4. When you do wrong, without knowing it, perhaps it may be excused. Especially if you are glad to be taught better.
5. But whatever Fault you commit willfully, knowing it to be a Fault, that cannot be excused.
6. So you must always be punished for lying, for calling Names. for Disobedience, or for striking any one.
7. For you know this is a Sin against God. And you must be punished for it, out of Love to you, and for your Good.
8. You deserve Punishment, both in the Sight of God and Man.
9. If this Fault was not punished now, it would grow upon you, and carry you to Hell.
10. To prevent this, it is good to let you suffer a Punishment now, a hundred thousand Million Times less than that.
11. If you do this again, you must be punished again, but pray to God that you may do it no more.
12. That foolish Love which would spare you now, would be indeed the most cruel Hatred.

Lesson XII
How to regulate our Practice

1. Some may think the Rules before laid down to be either impossible or ridiculous.
2. They would not appear impossible to us, but because we have not been accustomed to them.
3. If we had, we should find, by the Grace of God, that nothing can be easier.
4. Neither can any think them ridiculous, unless it be those to whom the Cross of Christ is Foolishness.
5. They are indeed ridiculous to the World, because the World is an Enemy to God.
6. But the Wisdom of the World is Foolishness with God, as the Wisdom of God is Foolishness to the World.
7. Therefore the Apostolic[27] faith, Know ye not, that the Friendship of the World is Enmity with God? Whoever therefore will be a Friend of the World, is the Enemy of God.
8. Be not conformable then to this present World.
9. And love not the World, nor the Things of the World. If any Man love the World, the Love of the Father is not in him.
10. How unhappy therefore are they, who bring up their Children according to the Rules of the World.
11. They who train them up, as it is called, to make their Fortunes in the World, to be great, rich, and honored in the World.
12. That is indeed, to perish with the World, to be turned into Hell, with all that forget God.

---

[27] Apostle.

13. They will be reproached and cursed to all Eternity, by those whom they thus trained up for the Devil, together with whom they will have their Lot in everlasting Burnings.
14. But happy are those, who despising the Rules of the diabolical and antichristian World,
15. Train up the precious Souls of their Children, wholly by the Rules of Jesus Christ.
16. They shall be blessed by them for ever in Heaven, and shall together bless God to all Eternity.

FINIS[28]

---

[28] This is the word used by Wesley to finish this work.

OTHER BOOKS BY THE AUTHOR

BIBLE STUDY GUIDES

1. **The Bible as Sacred History:** Survey of the Bible
2. **The Struggle with God:** Genesis through Deuteronomy
3. **Sacred Stories:** Joshua through Esther
4. **The Search for Wisdom:** Job through Ecclesiastes
5. **Time is Running Out:** Major and Minor Prophets
6. **Between the Testaments:** Books of the Apocrypha
7. **The Messengers:** The Four Gospels
8. **An Explosion of Faith:** Acts and Revelation
9. **The First E-Letters:** All of the Letters
10. **The Second Creation:** Revelation (Formatted: 6x9)
11. **A Vision of Hope:** Revelation: (Formatted 8.5x11)
12. **New Testament Photos 1**
13. **New Testament Photos 2**

BOOKS

1. **Ignited for Mission:** A Call to Missions
2. **Reformulating the Mission of the Church:** A Theology of Missions
3. **Our Spiritual Senses:** Five Spiritual Senses
4. **Our Spiritual Disciplines:** Six Spiritual Disciplines
5. **The Ordinary Christian Experience:** Fourteen Common Experiences
6. **Faith is a Choice:** Choosing Faith and Morality
7. **A Brief Story of the Christian Church:** A Survey of the Church
8. **The Heart of Methodism:** Renewing the Church

EDITED BY THE AUTHOR

1. **Foundational Documents:** Basic Methodist Documents
2. **Instructions for Children:** by John Wesley
3. **Speaking Iban:** by Burr Baughman
4. **The Essentials of Methodism:** Basic Methodist Beliefs

Printed in Great Britain
by Amazon